SPECTRUM®
READERS

LEVEL 1

COUNTRY!
Life on a Farm

By Teresa Domnauer

Carson-Dellosa
Publishing

SPECTRUM®

An imprint of Carson-Dellosa Publishing, LLC
P.O. Box 35665
Greensboro, NC 27425-5665

© 2014, Carson-Dellosa Publishing, LLC. Except as permitted under
the United States Copyright Act, no part of this publication may
be reproduced, stored, or distributed in any form or by any means
(mechanically, electronically, recording, etc.) without the prior written
consent of Carson-Dellosa Publishing, LLC. Spectrum is an imprint of
Carson-Dellosa Publishing, LLC.

carsondellosa.com

Printed in the USA. All rights reserved.
ISBN 978-1-4838-0112-4

01-002141120

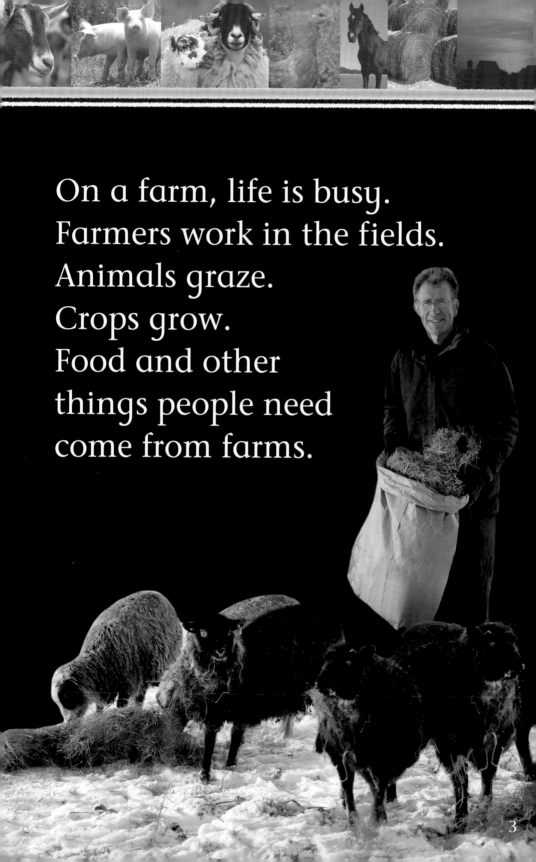

On a farm, life is busy.
Farmers work in the fields.
Animals graze.
Crops grow.
Food and other
things people need
come from farms.

Farmer

On a farm, you might
see a farmer.
Farmers work hard.
They plant fields and
care for animals.

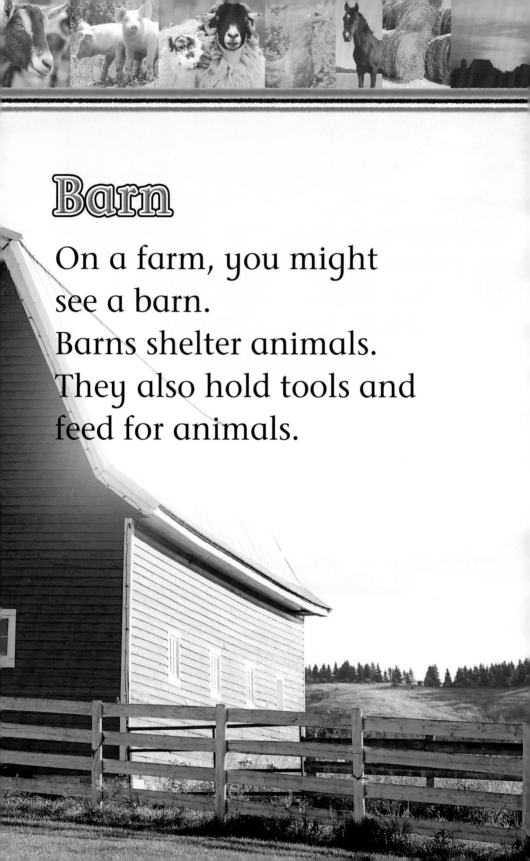

Barn

On a farm, you might
see a barn.
Barns shelter animals.
They also hold tools and
feed for animals.

Farm Machine

On a farm, you might
see a farm machine.
Big machines help farmers
plant and harvest crops.
This machine is called
a *combine*.

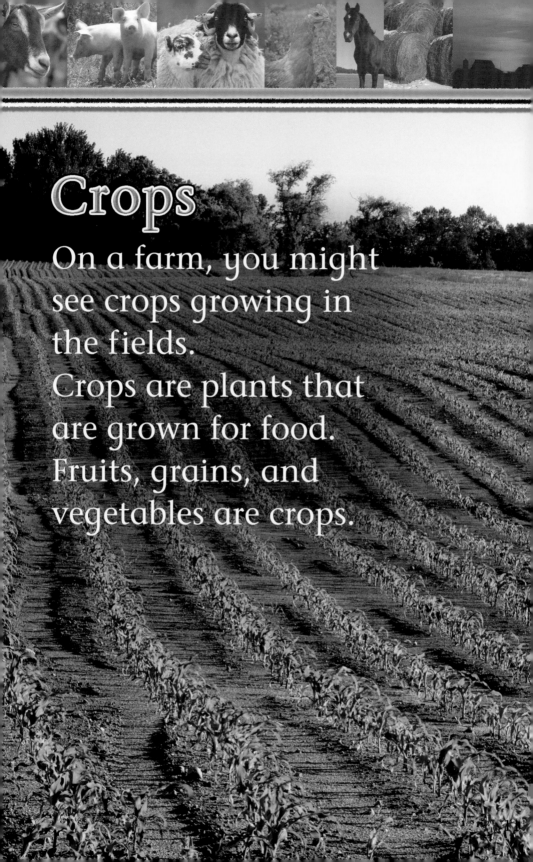

Crops

On a farm, you might
see crops growing in
the fields.
Crops are plants that
are grown for food.
Fruits, grains, and
vegetables are crops.

Corn

On a farm, you might
see tall stalks of corn.
Corn is an important crop.
It can be made into cereal,
tortillas, and other foods.

Farm Animals

On a farm, you might
see animals.
Farmers provide food, water,
and shelter for their animals.
Animals are raised for milk,
meat, and other products.

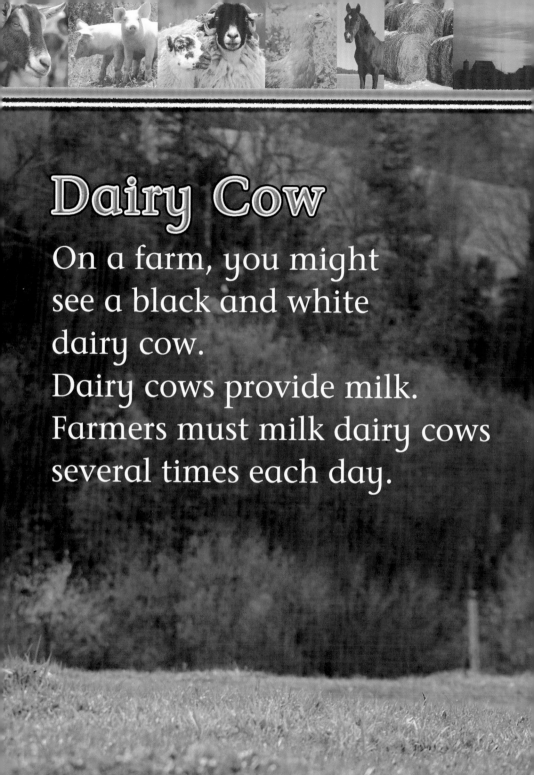

Dairy Cow

On a farm, you might
see a black and white
dairy cow.
Dairy cows provide milk.
Farmers must milk dairy cows
several times each day.

17

Goat

On a farm, you might
see a herd of goats.
Farmers raise goats for milk.
Some farmers number their
goats to keep track of them.

Pig

On a farm, you might
see pigs.
Piglets grow into
enormous hogs.
Farmers raise hogs for pork,
bacon, and other meat.

21

Sheep

On a farm, you might
see sheep.
Farmers raise sheep for
their wool.
People use wool to make
warm clothes and blankets.

Chicken

On a farm, you might
see chickens.
Farmers raise chickens
for eggs and meat.
The egg on your breakfast
plate came from a chicken.

Horse

On a farm, you might
see grazing horses.
Horses help farmers in
many ways.
They can carry people
and tools.

Hay

On a farm, you might
see bales of hay.
Hay is dried grass that
farmers feed to animals.
Farmers store hay for
animals to eat all
winter long.

Sunset

On a farm, you might see the sun go down after a long day. Farmers work from sunrise to sunset. Their hard work helps to feed many people.

COUNTRY! Life on a Farm
Comprehension Questions

1. Name three animals raised on farms.

2. What kinds of crops do farmers grow?

3. Why are farms important?

4. How do horses help farmers?

5. Why do farmers raise dairy cows?

6. What is wool used for?

7. Why do farmers raise chickens?

8. When do animals eat hay?

9. Why do farmers use machines?

10. What is a barn used for?